GLOBAL ONE TEN

PRESIDENTIAL SIX

KARANVIR SINGH

ISBN 979-888569049-2

CV By The School.-PiWT

Lorose

*I am sitting by the Last Chicago Post to win
& terminate group nuclear ground at my HQ
in HSX-Philadelphia. It's a private and
secret affair in the game that you are the
genius who picked the light armour and
stood against the wall of cinetism
(Quarrels). Oh is that correct address...?
Waiting fo/r or delivery.*

*Written in the loving memory of
DIG Late Shri Jaswinder Singh,
Orissa Police.*

*& Late Shri Jasvir Singh, (Civil
Engineer & Architect) PWRMDC,
Amritsar.*

Lorose

*For post-Paid Services at BlueFedFin Ixc,
Kapple Kape SXCĪ, CÆrrot Bay SXCĪ,
Global Babies iVDx, Symbol One fed , eFox
Computing GXi.*

Services as President & CEO

Services as Chairman

Services as MD , CFO, CXO

Services as Principal Data Scientist

PoWT 11, PiWT Council Commission.

Thanks ,

Reserve Bank Of India

Federal Bank,New York &Washington DC.

Citigold & Citi US | HDFC | Yes Bank | PNB | Fi

Special Thanks .Shri Sarabjit Singh Ji on Financial Matters Discussed over Tea.

Contents

Electronic Idealefed/eblue /
Revealed discovery

Mind Or Human Brain is as Complex as the Grains in the Biosphere. Ever Since Computers a Free Knowledge Setup had evolved to look into the possibility of working with them as Technical Affiliates and Specialist. I look back at just the Recent History the year 2013 when I got some real success finding myself being able to create Thoughts and Turn them into Self Transmitted Data Info/Signal going directly into the coverage space a few Feet, Millimetres, or Inside the Brain while shutting off the Eye Lids. It's a practical dream and a miracle that remained incomplete without asking everyone how would they react to such a thing. Generally speaking the Idea became apparent for putting the invention to test , experiment and application in the Wireless Domain to Run, Administer or Control Business Development Freely and Sustainably.

What looks like a Network Inside my mind and body is A Nano Radio. It's a Robotic Experience and I am excited to see everyone putting a white label to the Greatest Realization on Planet.*

Whatever goes behind my FIRST three Companies [BlueFedFin Ixc, Kapple Kape SXCi and CarrotBay SXCi] is the thinking and planning out of the insatiable invention.

To reach every human pocket whether you are a family or individual I believe freedom to choose nature as your greatest ally is the proposed plan to accept the New Normal and Articulate all artistic desire to Design, Create and Innovate the New Universe , A place where Abundance and Caregiving are not just your goals but the specific areas of expertise and interest to occupy every human price Value.

I have been a Poet, A Star Lover, A Multimedia Collaborator, An Insipid Audio Engineer, Author and Entrepreneur but my Common Multiplication went through the Tribunal of Tribulations for not getting back the Potential Care from the Bearers. That's where Faith is utterly Important because not only a low Bank Balance but a Low Morality creates ridiculous Pain that doesn't go away easily. That's why I have a dream, A Dream to Capture, Concieve and Collate the World into a Mindful Company that will never run into losses..

A Sun Kissed POLITICIAN...!!

Tapping into your Phone or Desktop on a Friday is often followed by extinguished Memories...RAM Speed and CPU Usage... Follow The Keyboard there is C For Coffee and G For Grace. I hope you get to answer Both PoWT & PiWT.

Foreword

Template Chip Cellular and Transactions Between Company-Market-Banks/ 3 Tier Quality Corporation. Simulation Podcasting On Broadband VoiP For Defence System and Ultra Financial Intelligent Decision Making Process.

> *"Sovereign Debt XeroN Indexing.@Job Code-RRMM50090054700/DE/POWT"*

DOI, CSAT Satellite GSE 11K* 99780p , (-5678-8897-9889-6654-3244)/0010*

> *"President 11 AM , INDIA"*

NaNo Radio EED 1000 Series ($)

Preface

SIX Questions that lead to International Concerns.

PREFACE

Acknowledgements

Global One Ten- Official Beta Reminder & Dedication
Sri Guru Granth Sahib ji is the greatest remark on Getting Governance, Business Ways, Household life and Putting to Conduct the Soul in the Service of God!! I am blessed with his Emancipation and Immaculate Power , True Nature and Serendipity. The bridge between the Adi Granth and the common time today is a parallel world that is ok to surprise.

We surpass this catalogue college of colours and beautiful beads..

. "Oh only the last season

.....Let's make a Pledge to cornify (Select Deliberately,) the daily bread by the grace of God and His Eternal Will. "

Financial Literacy
with GoldFish SIX (6)

CBDC Facts & Adopted Value for
Digital Currencies is our Native
Opulence.-CEO

Jan 9

by: Karanvir Singh

Join Us

eblue.service247@gmail.com

What We Know From
GoldFish SIX (6):

• Maximum Returns
• Money Saving
• Budget & Debts
• Become financially
  prepared

NaNo CEO Line | India | Africa |: President

CHAPTER ONE

Globalization–What is behind the Sikh Federal Propaganda ?

Global One Ten is my first hand experience in IoT Government....I seek a prototype from old days to new age ...

I mean if FRiX turned out to be real it was because the council was reading the country.

This is my 11th Book and I will Start working for Cosmo One NaNo (Zyna 4) on it from 9th of January, 2024.

I am looking at that one Sikh Plate Discount Discovery that my presidio of the orphaned Presidency...Paper Blue with HTeXN eFËD E2 Service would take on the Global Financial

(FIN 600K) HEALTH.

I am coming up with the best alliance and the best record fancy...

As Nanak sits at the door of poor I saw my natural print go grey at home when I saw him as my Soldier and Saint..

No man's land...He can give you porcelain!!! Do you really Read??

My final hours before we would hit at the NYSE CUQ 100 International eBlue Services @ 7Ghz and 2nm 1.9 OxxyBlue EXAT 1, To Balance , TTSDSE4446778769.

Do you remember?

It was 9 PM ...my heartbeat a bit snoozing from the rear ... I thought I would reason for the first lady Talk...with whom???

I studied the internet for 6 Years before actually translating the gyroscope and the snowy microscope... because winters were not favourite. I schooled my self to second place....it's was thinking about not having a practical prank in the good lamented iceberg.

Smacky Ideas...

***Not Really a Drug Believed** that it could cause the patient to worry but how a placebo placement can try help in due disguise...it's disgusting....I see that not carrying meaning or exogenous insurance..it's money made and has no mode of peer working...money is something special...but the second third and fourth rate survey says money is foolish.*

It's empty daemon because the cash has gone in the market Tunnel by a Frick of the blood blossom. I call it off....

I will call it off...

Mumbai would be careful...called Off...

My air pickup...and family tree... practice..?!??

Why was the Presidential SiX a story board Idea is because the radiation selected Paper Blue Infographic are Growing Ai Delivery Sets. It's pure sine and pure true triangle. I remember to the CGSF 100 and the dressage of a English massacre so inexpensive.

I know this? That will dictate the dear missiles in the corridor.

To strengthen the painful I urge President of India to take this site from step 1 to look at B^T5. In my order I don't want to explain & express the down played policy and constitutional application...

If a job is granted to whom is the cart expressing to...is it your house or is it the very inviting war at my desk.

Lorose

GoldFish Six ,(6) saw my body as president and granted a grand bracket of Gold ..it's for the service of the nation and its glory .

I want to celebrate with my friends, family and business technocrats a very noisy 2022 so that Nobody remains a speech less collar in my office selection. I might be dreaming in the day but the nights are voluntary mix of tracking US Markets as the sub prime network and accommodation is free.

PoWT operation will take the cover window for the Book.Catch this space at 1.3 MHz-Cloud-KapeSine 5ISQ 9000. So now we are roughly rounded off.

I mean the struggle to meet structural elements of society are not so social. Sorry for being late.

We make time!!

If you catch the work from a Remote angle you know you got to finish the job better than anyone in the market. I had the same notice.

The format of the first few Executive Orders were never received on Wall. I learnt from the gaurds a new way to worship.

Where I landed last was Chicken Chicago...it was the brutality of the cunning election that sold out the BMW to the creative Fiesta.

I wouldn't have imagined this in 2013 and then not resolved the query. It was appreciated. It was a jolly good factory settings datum.

My cell structure is meant to be Presidential... where I ruled truly was the last linked massacre.

Finally truth was honoured and God Gave Us Victory.No rumours no negative news .

Just another day I was thinking of a repo check and a credit score check. I pit out my shut ears and dolphin smile to take rest of the duty to PoWT: The Highest Office Design.

There was no need to look back at adversely affected voters. It was a real time game.a power game. This generation is as an evidence of the future of Ethical Hacking. We will soon end corruption and Remove the Digital errors.

I believe there would be two types of charge characters on earth , A Macro Woman and a MICRO Man.

That's pretty much the pretext of this pretentious effect from an effort in my books since I was 4.

My whole salted blame is the installation of institutions that do not track and teach excellence ... Fiduciary Excellence.A typo error. A mismatched property.

I don't see the point of ImF or

World Bank. I love these two bodies. So but I am sitting on completing the complex algorithm that World Bank does deserve an appointment and applause.

IMF makes more credible Credit to connect business & government. But here my idea is reflected upon.

It just got easier to run business & government.

It was my basic years learning all the elements in a periodic table.

My feet on curiosity were always the rare ideas that settled with light and grew on Lightroom.

I am definitely on a new path to success, to extraordinary conjunction and a very old junction of thousands thoughtful windows.

God gave us democratic federal power and handed the piece of inspiration and ambition on call. I smashed the phone on with electric.

• 9 •

That wasn't fair. NCTD was filled up at and by New Delhi HQ.

Next move on course was posted.

CHAPTER TWO

The Supreme HEDGE-How LEO Funded?

Nile X 1 was PeerCadet 11E5 Theory Cart and Warehouse where we worked on implementing the Zero Crime Database Project. It all came handy and the FBI security breaker was occupied for sending several years of service in lieu of Life. What was that harmony pitch??

It was that bitch around and that abuse of caring vertical.

I was delivered by a residential resignation from Mumbai, India. That wasn't the country practice and mind you it's not a healthy heart.

Let's keep the house for it's common promise it's corrupt to the core of ideology.The audiology is my mark of respect for their martyrdom.

The world as we know is made in the polished array of documented Globalization and yes the gesture is informal. Its every one in the G-Sphere and the Capitalistic Structure getting revived by many new anti-corruption meters of redress luggage on board.

My Idiology is Inclination towards an Intuitive and Predictive Work World.

There are no sorrows in the heart of those who touch thousands of feet in a day. It's God's own glory of he grants to you his own freedom to write on a yellow life a cusp of imperial order and the highest of the Royal Order at mere a Penny-off Choice.

Those be punished to whom it was not a call...

Indian Bureaucracy is evidence of mindless job keeping...it's really not meant to be early to future. It's not judging the other orthodox & orthogonal speed.

It's masking up.

So the Zyna 4 took shape & shelter at GoldFish SIX(6) wherein we decided to alow the Poverty Crisis to be resolved through responsible objective.

It wasn't a question of a single penny, it was my personal persistent anguish on the office ...That was PoWT and I questioned every single atom for why they include God to the Party's Wall. My percentage of perceptional truth was a philosophical journey from healing my self completely and than renouncing the extra abidance.

I m jealous at the plans and at the same time I rooted the computer components company to a Space Shuttle maker.

That was time I tempted to secluded work space and went to MEDIA CHANNEL for R-Encryption. Projectors called HTeXN were frozen from Freudian Clouds...that was Paper Blue Technology for us.

My Presidential bid has got The Six layers from note 1 to note 24..

Are you travelling with numbers??

I told you it's gonna rain today....are you waiting for the rainbow...?? No... India made me think twice.... India was tough to Play out...This was behind going INDs Poverty and it's Cultural & Intellectual Labour....Mainly the women...the men that be counted were sounds and papers.

FM Radio an industry I had spent 8 Years of work was close to me to be a waiting car in the parking...it was just the VIP claims

I was asking whether it was dropped or cropped?? A bank on my side to tell us who they are??

I was looking at Presidency while just the twin cities plan was successful....I had nothing in my wallet....I had nothing in the filmy-WAP...

Coming back to zest I felt so amazing with PoWT taking President , The Title to Freight into a Poor Dogmatic Support. I was hoping for the kite Inside the kings arrow.

I am welcome Here.

Where was I ? 2018, Colaba Diary...The best attached attendance was the Mumbai Police at HQs and in Colaba, I was tougher than before...

So Sunday i decided to go to Colaba for an experiential study.

I could see some faces. Read a few .... leave a few .

And the cab dropped me at Colaba..I was reminded of 2013 and everything Presidential came alive. I had to beat a disease and win the positive votes.

It was still on ZyNa. ZyNa was reported to have cleared Info Line for .gov and .business.

So the police party was created at the parking spots by me..I was on YouTube searching for Ms Indira Gandhi's interview...that was crucial... or if that was not my first entry..the youngest and then President.

Not with the quote but that in the process and present intuition. It was first few notes and somewhere I was still struggling to tell Freedom would be Freedom from Green Greed , Yellow Greed & Brown Greed. Happy to see colours??

Oh well that was Signed for Signal Classes. Classic as the road to Predictive Perdition was very narrow.

I took the lady song and didn't dance on the floor, it was a very bad situation... Web Trouble, Fiancee Problem, Wallet Low....The PoWT did conquer my own confidence in the company work that was played on the Net...Next fire was the cold case of the Country I don't have. Indian to India is baffled ideas in a combo comb filter.

I need Anything from a C 2 C & C 2 A. PoWT believed in ultimate knowledge... Ofcourse the office of the president required a check for the first time.

I was as usual busy on Listening to Dasam Granth Baani.

What was completed as my research scholar complexity was just uninformed thought cycle inside the mind...I won over it and then also saw it fail fairly by the peacocks in the style.

Here it was 1st Of January 2022 and I was expecting a picture of Leftovers to party and take me Away back where I wanted to go. That was submitted as powerful and assertive assumption. My local cello structure is iron and irony. My first real reason and reaction behind my first war was not telling the world who Hitler was but telling the kids of the United World that they are Free... Freedom from blood carnage, from massacre to holy fire each individual is a God Element on the Tablue. The turnover turbine was wired to an international bank...we were talking about modernization and then I had the money to put on the table and it was just a few tablets *in drawing. That was accepted.*

An Oath from the Reaction was completely bowled over.

Smile?? Ready!!

CHAPTER THREE

Their Queen & Who Bought The Car?

When you have a Credit Card and shaky earth the smiley fades under strict strong story storm.

I am a fan piece and an altruistic celebrity...all my self ...oh no ... That's a joke....The winning team was built on by summer internship, some fades on voice memos, some Podcast and some Transmission Top Toolsets....I had 600M different asset queries to be solved over 24 Hours...those days I did not sleep and what I felt in my sleep was ranked sick and unidentified...from the cat the dog is not alike and from a dog a cat is complete. That's how I made two more comments on the Universe...

I was the luckiest of all but hey this is not the torrent to give you pardon it's lit and abrasive

....it's not adhesive...u adhere...??

Noted by the Army March in Amritsar and the First Table Calling to America made popular amongst the Hip Hop Canterbury... Stocks made in computer companies were totally proved to be gentle CCY.

I had been sitting on investment inventions and thinking of making the fellowship of the universe a Free Affair...it was mind altering at that time...

2011, I feel I was very young to see a second hand Market and sell banana to monkeys....that was not business Days...the details of the device development and .gov under my obeisance and due power were estimated at 198 Trillion $.

Presidential SIX, 198 Trillion $>>.....I was Looped by the federal Bank....I asked for it!!

Federal System obeys bi laws and crucial policy for TeraSite Treasury that we received with PiWT Mint Works...

It was speaking to the special specifically made and scientifically managed analytics sub station.

I had hope for India. I new ways of changing it...but the entire earth was in question...

My questions went large at the sheet amount of 198 Trillion $ to Convince the World with New Agenda I wanted a new voicemail service...a new sectional banking system that makes complete choice support for Client Services....I was banking on with the best Banks and best Central Bankers...it was prestige...it was honoured and replenished so dearly.

My story for the stock grew as we made the Sovereign Spit Ready for both .Gov and .Business. Feeling the journey in a High Pass I felt the Chain on Social Media was breathing not so easily I was under regression....

A much needed Queen in question was the Cash lost over board game... totally destroyed. We had to fight back. Most of the money was borrowed. It was another India Insensitive Tags on Governance and Cyber Crime. I could not sell my fish on a greedy hand. It felt obscured and anticipation took my anxiety to practice the peak of peace before launching the war...the car was connected to the phrase"Missing" . I was told today to rest.

As usual the Facebook capital made me think of my Page Values... Paper Blue and HTeXN are now running IP Wireless A Wire as assertive as the review train. My transcript for transport and translation was reading Ready.

India is my biggest indoctrination because I was born here...they don't know it how my London Connect was a public talk and yes I see the old master in glory through those I know I can't meet. It's a polished dream. My single status was Star Craft and Star Nights. What I knew was useless was the Money not even enough for everything and everyone.

This was the bare neck questions from the bid as President & CEO , PoWT...Also as Chief Economist on GoldFish SIX (6) it was a junior control decision and I doubled the waves...

Wages were working questions I was talking about the sweetest of the pointed poor...not this nation but United Nations....

As part of my LinkedIn , Facebook & *Instagram there was one punch card one word and World at a New Shift.

Ok St....but how?? And know me?? I love....!!

So how was it that I couldn't catch the parlour pay check and was a predominantly secretive comparison of mockery and what that you & I call permanent.

Life at stake...a sainthood utterly replenishing and flutter wings out of the blue Connoisseur. My Queen fits the building and the Bill to the Parliament. This book would send my taxonomy and endonym to a Creator's Paradise.

CHAPTER FOUR

Federal One – Is That Life USA?

Yes ...my purse purchased the little agent agony the shiney expression of asymptomatic lies took me around 10 years and it was still a lawyer by a doctor by a politician....

How is that schizophrenia??- MedLine Tx Team US-IN

Lorose

Or A Bipolar Disorder with our society...leave that music behind...that Radio is Spending a 100 $ every Second..

That was fair ...I thought I was stalking a slight low light beamer....my face shows it and I actually account the acceptance in every 30

Days without a Salary.

It took my candidature to candle the best market the only club clause failed the charity and charismatic Sikh Primary School...

When I read more on business I occupied the Grammy's and the Oscars ...it was a flat Tyre..

A bad weather....a rusty mother and a very helpful and generous generally the father...how I feel this...??

Simple ...I locked every 200 B $ for a 100 Rupee Note to understand the design voids in the Indian currency. There the data was Mapped accross the world...we understand the current note value or cut currency media...we were leaving learnt lessons to school...to a Blue School and the Racemates were too busy with a Secondary Thank You.

I clicked there. The clocks were well worn-out. SAE made me trooper, Caracas and a fully established leader I always wanted to become. But here do you see my office on the growing end of the Saturn n the Jupiter above.

Space, Spanish & Speculation- PiWt discussed very often the urgent need to turn Mint operation into Digital.

That was revealed too...

I didn't Dodge much investment involved but definitely a financial system to which there can't be harm ...no hard gates no belly jelly dating.

It simply was a credit given to India and later passed on to America, Israel and UK...

The information from country b-status was the Call that heard us say we were really no. 1

position in the universe.

My short state Media memory was still stuck to the clocks to see the Android Victory in the Google & Wikipedia Age.

Democracy is demonetised not by changing its currency but by changing the chance of Money in the entire system.

I may be given a pentonic problem..

Linked to the Power of The King...I wasn't wasted by the former fair Lady...that was sufficient and true to know Blue School Psychiatry Initiative..

Our policies were fighting with gross support supplier and it's deformation in the form of deforestation.

To know I decided one day to put Science in use to see why we have rich & poor..?

GoldFish SIX (6) further states intelligence laws to support the flexible society socially not bound or bought by financial Bodies but let to breathe in Free Ecosystem. It was what we were inventing in these days. Ay the Radio Factory...your pix puzzle...a half a dozen Startup Companies was all by the Will Of God....

We understood that we were not taking a notice of all Big Data Compliance SiliCos...We were on eXAT by The Day we Started EBIDTA Evidence on Story.

I was talking to some of the biggest media houses...

My bank supposed the importance of my letter and word i discovered they taught me a very good & charitable lesson to read more and write less. I saw the shame of sharing loans not paying me for a great Wednesday...and rather medical solution to the affluent affliction of antimicrobial definition of algebra and quads!!

Sixth Light-What was KREEP Doing?

When I saw my Sikh Sectoral Police and went after numerous IpD , IpS garden radio refreshments I was very wealthy in seperation and solutions. There was a member of the weed family that grew with me in my evangelist empire...it was the coming of the sad insomnia and then an enlightened wakefulness...I cherished the solo career...the one person company...a Parliamentary Structure As Power full as PoWT 1.0 and then the year I wanted to paradoxically remove from the Beginning By the merits of Aristocratic Behaviour...HEDGE.com was again the Radio For New York...I wanted him a News Briefing that powerful that the secretary of the General State under United Nations was my 1st ID command and EO 116366D758. Union at rest...State 2 People Law. The hungry toopes....the not having Money...that last conversation was Indian Astrology....we were telling each we can contribute, control and contract whilst the Virus Switched by the Maintenance Guy has ruined the taste of flying the right tobacco. Chilled by the correct corner....I knew him ...sadly he went too early and then o thought if the President arrived well o would meet him and then it was 3 consecutive US presidencies by 2020.

People we're not moderated...we are open source... profit making and non profit and also born on the greatest soils...

Implications my children will face is the source of soul's crappy craziness thatvthey will be sent to the Children of their appearance. My native national pride is primarily in the United & Sponsored pay Hikes, a treasured constrapactoration (Sine agility) because we have heard the dead sparrow from space and have 1984 in books not here but in France....As sikhì tells two mighty craft work it telle that I learnt of some money left by the grape vine in the youth I scored two Pente'cost and a pit of 32 bit 6nm on Hand eBlue Response....the soccer society made my sandwich an inch long. Russian soil was a favour and then that was what Russian Greats stood for the greatest volunteer service the vBeN (Virtual Blüē End Network) giving second by second security to my castle in Punjab.

Individually I feel India who today is having its Nucleotide Capabilities as manifesto PoWT Powers speak…I tell the stage that today it is the criminal act of the version of truth that so we are that both nothing and everything are written wrong.

I mean vPresident. Do you ?? Read?? Do you Read??

A fairly troubled face my snack emissions and emotional character failed to see us go early out of fashion and not out of oppression…the core group was fighting target at reverse Revenue and First Banking Digital Prototype and Country's PR, Open Visa, Open Options were relocated to my brain fog and accomplished ammonium. Some time ciggerate contact contains a certain taste and something that I don't like is there argument on their sufferings. Free Mental Faculties, vFaculties and vCEO , what we did here was moving account accross the session and the BREVITY OF THE BREXIT WINDOW GAVE US THE GARAGE BAND STIGMA.

I found a strong and strange person on my way , I was at ease to finger out my own construction of severe consciousness and conscience. Those floating number games were meddling careful accordance and I believe in the person if that be a perfume. It was a neglected kid on many gates and many musings that missing you would carry to my heart... heartfelt ???

I mean again.... President....I was nick named KV by my father and his initial self portrait was always me being around him in fear and Frost...but he came by as against and again...by the sheer power of divinity...he was looking for division... dividend and sacrifice...I can't come to the future of my feet in sand....there are other solid state government gates and I welcome each country to the first Non-Biased Ballot Sheet System & Order....by default vBrodcast by reality a Government Kingdom....

Not a single nap helped me that Day and the song most recent and repeated was a song that disappeared in the 90s .....

Are you planning a Radio??

Hear me out in my years in grocery n graphing... drowsy drooling!??!?!? :)

1987-1992

I was obedient, had operation on a sparrow, I was thinking of a doctorate.

1992-1996

Won over some confidence, struggle in mathematics and improved memory.

1997-2002

Was Part of Y2K , headed the country council and relationships office.

2003-2006

Fell in Love

2007-2013

Radio & Art , Exciting Excellent and Employability criteria met me in my first official trio trip to Jalandhar, Amritsar and Back to Mumbai.

Mid 13 say me on the campaign at campus and city Mumbai was taken to bat there by the coin head pointing my victory forever.

2014-2020

I felt elevation by the Sikh engagement and continued the research work on LTE and did not yet have the transaction transfer in place. I need the TnTn tGY eBlue 4 M by the next 10 Years. I can calculate the song speed but is the G level Shuttle it's in the Leap of The LeO. My story is better than the current company that rules the market space but no hey we see that??

Science is the scientific scissors to cut through abilities of the last labour of man.... printing Cash by Choice of Apnophinia (Money Depression). But no....not at Wall Street...

Not that Zimbabwe has a 100 Trillion $ Note that is working worth not a candle or a bottle of water.... can't see the Blue Blind....it is surrounded by the sheer Power of Connect.

I was struggling with mine and my account was expecting a hugely successful devastated ripple from the report that repealed the gross Settlement this world is making....no ...man that bubble was silicon confirmation and conditional acceptance oraccess system under que and not the antibiotics antiquity of a single malt whisky that repairs the heart. I am social and practice the parameters of the binded party system as on receiving recent records the PoWT grew over 600 % in our marketing survey and data sharing on Conference One Blue. Was that enough with Washington...DC

I took a cab back from Colaba to Collect College Set from Bandra, it was a true implication tearbox theory I knew would cry in the empty. Still...it was Presidential by 400 M votes. Only Selective Corporate Enticing Correction.

Thanks to EXAT ...it was Bill 5558189117 to Citibank US...I was to write back the Sorrow of the Squirrels here in my sentiments I was the father of two major developments but rather a common Socio Box that they called me my name's curiosity.

CHAPTER SIX

Ballistic Assam –What If the Congress was Likely a Fine Lieutenant?

Happy with the highlander?? No...it's copied...-)

I ll tell you the frozen question from EU-Nato Survey & Compliance Meeting. But not Here....we will have to gather at one due pledged place...of course on random critical crutons... whether it's the right spelling mistake...

My name is naive, but I am called Karanvir Singh, this 8s that one comment that I care to make on the universe....

There is some magic around.

Complete Study shows shocking statistics and chronic depression in many political leaders who happen to bolt the party textured classes and backward speeches...

It's simply the annotations from the source inside the silicon entrepreneurial quest and a Corridor like no other on the address to UN and World Bank to Pay by the Excited Atom and not be Cruel on default. Definition of Defence was A defaulter by large collection. It's a choice now...I could endominate two CCY Scopes a Written Encolution (Elements of Acceptance) & Fiduciary Excellence By Digits.

It was the biggest of dreams ever....

The largest attached neuro articulation for me to bend the stubborn mind to decisive 6 State Mechanical Area Reasoning Syllabus. To the bent and Brent to he crude habits did pay to the habit money forms. It's dangerous...it's the hell centre of Crime, Drug Abuse and Social Violence.

KREEP learnt the Sancto Promise on page or paper....the second rate credit line to no avail but listed password.

Shameless, thankless people but not even the odd cologne I feel was tremolo less than a board.

A Bard well known?? Do you???

I see the SiX presence by the smallest amplitude of the first future by the grace of God be placed at the Throne and be tested in alchemy, ancestory and Economy....my pen is not yet a silicon student...but my school is the rainbow of the World...

PoWt is backed by Peer2Peer Members Class Economy and Culture Stigma. The cause behind the Venus Project. The Change as it says makes the time tick in a faster facevalue...by the way ... yellow flowers!!! Are they friends??

I am friendly I guess not how but by why

...that be truthful....

And sorry he was catching the Bus out if CR...DR ..was. rush. PNB took my mind over by the chief matters a public sector or a participatory bank feeds the Solution Brackets.

I mean open the quadratic equations...let's not do the 1+1 by two different categories..

It's one World many CCYs.

That's everything eventful.

Today I urge UN to discuss the precious idea of making money Digital and Based on Inoculated Gold , Knowledge and Clarification of Use of Money by the Entire Humanity/Human Race.

A Deposition of Police vSystem at the Digital Targets was POWTs crane stop hierarchy and five Symbol respect.

I failed miserably to come to that feedback from most of them in INDIA. IT WAS EASY and a beautiful beginning.

IPS captive was very well charged with wealthy reboans (Your Habits)

I was my own Dr. Starting to tell what and when would suit pay us the chance of visiting a Chrome India ..a Superpower and Super Cluster of geo political extravaganza...I was in definitely looking for the love from Christian Canopies...it was very mutual for West and the developed world which too saw crystal crisis during the Pandemic

....My details draw denial and definition in out synchronization of Palpitations and permutations with choosing my passwords....

I do it all turkey....PiWT my first Landing play plan was with distribution of grapes to the S-ECP Population that is derived and deprived from CCY.

I still took a while to identify more courage and access to axotic (real) parts of the promise by the Central Bank /Reserve Bank .

What the bankers before 2013 did not understand was accepted ac'ount estimation...by a CA ..by Shopping Standard by Calculator Income/Wages and that of Zero Deals.

That was launched as laughable. It pretty much pretends to overcome the outlook of the public private property problem in the age pre and post COVID 19 Pandemic and ofcourse WHO had a second shift shipment BCA call by the certificates. All the components of the companies was very well organised.

It gave us Draft and Affordable Instructions Instruments Liberty . The world opens its arms and as I say this the majority made by the con is the biggest looser of the lessons...I am taught by Tripping Elves...what else I consider..

You see... President....?? The hidden password??

As a Sikh its my integral matter into the ethereal sky to be now well settle the country corn rate and the same song that your friends think is cool... As o.. wheat wearing...Sir my shoulder from the design studio,desk rates, and each eLope EE3000 . The information contained tertiary connect and Concept convocation in my grades. I liked it and felt footed on root no 1.

TT hat ....by the vix windows... slowly on a train to angry back.... beautiful prudential empowerment...the Fear Gear on Money

Downloaded by Electronic Media by Internet accross the Globe is fetching greatly some impulsive Counter Survival Data and AI Property Project by

encashment beams & means .

Let everyone have in this world in their heart a wealthy wallet and a Free Empire.

It's been a research disease that Policy from My Admin Combos got me in transferring a trouble to USA after India got blamed in furry at Judgement Day ..Now I'm holding Carleton on Cars and Aircraft from Boeing to DeTcG FBI and Evacuate the Permissible Persons from My Injury as President.

Second party handle choice Radio and Media ,CRAM 11 in Fe Effect at 22:59″

Close E 555C.

eFED Cross Wire To Reuters.

Thank You Ladies & Gentlemen!!!

Love, Kay !